APPRECIATE THE BUTTERFLIES

Also by Joey Groves

Tangerine: Or, How I Learned to Trust the Process

APPRECIATE THE BUTTERFLIES

JOEY GROVES

ILLUSTRATED BY
LISA SUMIKO STEWARD

www.grooovy.co

For my Mother, who wants me to live a peaceful life

Contents

PORTRAITS

Introduction

It's been four years since I published *Tangerine: Or How I Learned to Trust the Process*, and now I'm thrilled to share my latest poetry collection with you: *Appreciate The Butterflies*. This is the rawest, angriest, and most personal story I've ever written, and I find myself wondering if people will relate to it—or even care. With that being said, I don't think I have it in me to write something as candid as this in the future.

Something inside me pushed me to create this, almost like I was possessed. At first, I brushed it off, but the feeling grew exponentially until one night, I found myself up late, writing poems from midnight until 5am. It was like a dam had burst; I simply couldn't stop.

The title, *Appreciate The Butterflies*, stems from a conversation I had with my good friend, Brice, in 2021. I was talking about my dreams, aspirations, and all the things I wanted to achieve by a certain age, overwhelming both myself and her. In response, she told me to slow down, to "appreciate the butterflies" before they go. That phrase has stuck with me ever since, reminding me to be present and control the breath. Not long ago, I read something that resonated with me deeply: "Butterflies stop and rest when it rains because it damages their wings. It's okay to rest during the storms of life—you'll fly again when it's over." It's a testament to how important rest is, how we should give ourselves more grace in a world that demands constant perfection and how we should let go of the burdens of expectations.

Over the past four years, I've experienced the full force of the human condition. Grief, apathy, guilt, shame—these emotions became my closest companions. In life, I've lived with them and learned from them; in this collection, I've explored them deeply.

Now, as I prepare to release these words into the world, I feel both anxious and excited. Once this book is out, it no longer belongs to me—it belongs to you, the reader. So don't forget to *Appreciate The Butterflies* ~

Joey Groves
16 October 2024

DAYS OF
INNOCENCE

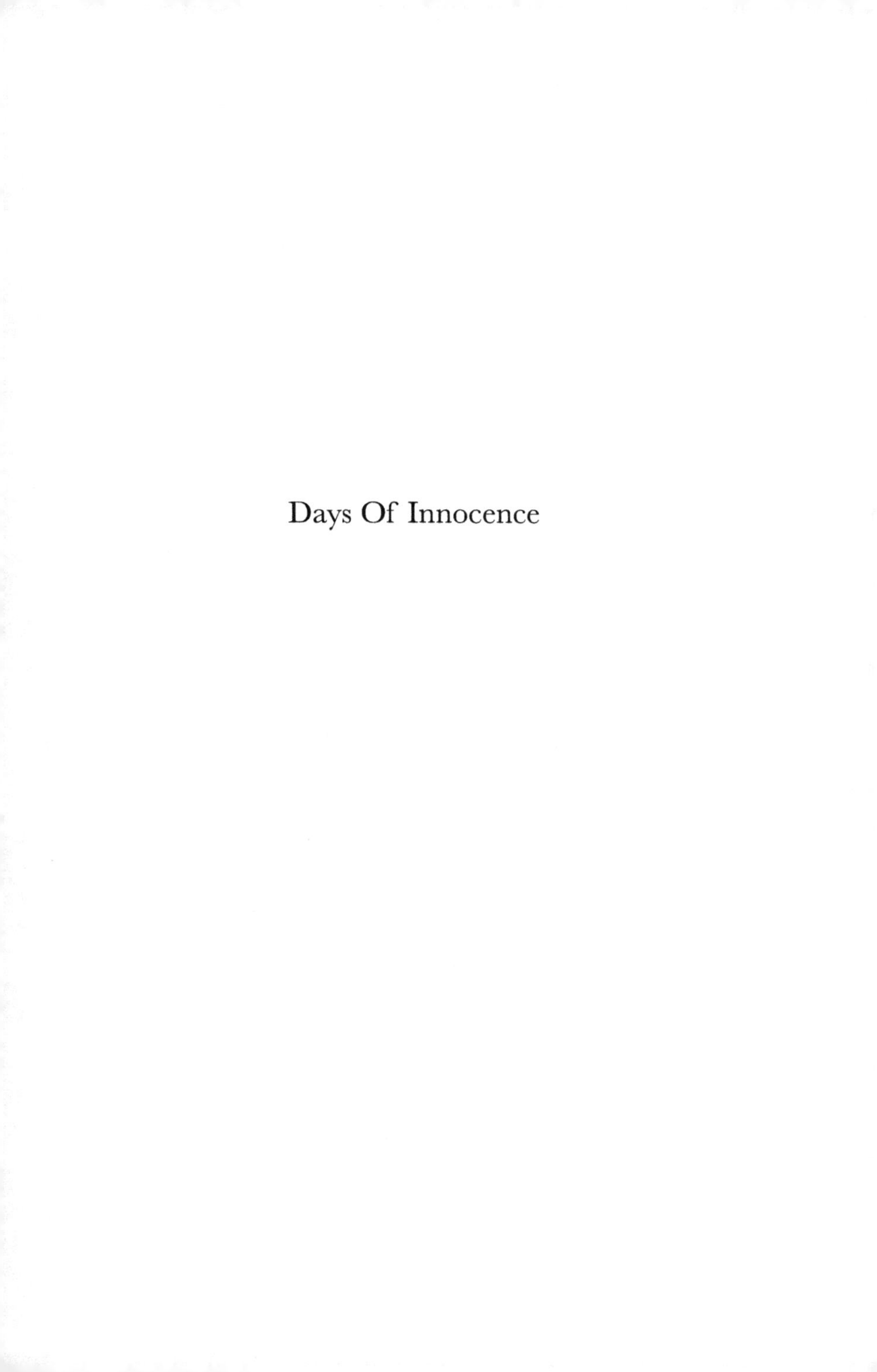

Days Of Innocence

Kabukicho

I don't get it
I had dreams here
naivety or hope,
call it whatever

one thing I was conquering:
fear

I should have
run away
with her
to the ends of
the Earth

But little did I know

how?

how can i know
that i'll be alright in the near future?
how do i know that i can trust my friends?
how many more books and songs do i need to write
until i'm satisfied?
so i can die peacefully
how many followers and praise do i need to love myself?
how can i find love if i don't know what it is i'm looking
for?
how can i be happy?
how can i not be angry?
how can i be okay tomorrow?
how?!
is there anybody out there?

Kendal Mint Cake

Sometimes I think
that you're just away from home
in one of your ski holidays
with my brothers and sisters;
Or you're in one of your
weekend excursions, walking the Peak District;
In either case I can't wait for you
to bring me back some Swiss chocolate
or some Kendal Mint Cake

Sometimes I think you're in your chalet,
the wooden Swiss shack
you built all by yourself;
From the concrete block foundations
to the carpet
you laid it all by yourself

You're working away on the computer,
which happens to be
the first PC I built all by myself;
I still remember
the pungent smell of coffee or tea

And I'm staring at the wall
where university plaques hung;
Hoping that, I would,
one day have my plaque on the wall too

Days keep happening

Days keep happening
Oh so lovely!
So much to do, yet,
I'm not here

Tired of routine:
trapped under the
thumb of fear

frolicking

frolicking around
looking good on film
now i'm wondering
if i'm living for the moment
or for the future

Fail!

only twenty,
and yet I act like
my neck is on the line

the pen is heavy,
i'm ready to fail;
wondering if i'll
ever reach
my prime

May I have this dance?

I'm longing to connect
because I know
how alone
we (really) are
pretending we're not
in this cosmic trance

Hence why
I'll always have
this dance

She spoiled it all

We talked all night
I'm dreaming lucid,
she said
something stupid

Shot down by cupid;
forgot to breathe
she planted seeds
then dug 'em up

She left me here:
I live in fear,
(I cried)
my mind's clear
of being behind
in mere seconds

Something in the universe

I feel cosmically alone

I keep forgetting there's a pandemic
outside

I hear her moan

She lied

My sleeved heart I shouldn't have shown

It reminds of me of why
she's not my kind

Too much!

I feel so lost!
I have too much shit
going on

The cost of dealings
with Baphomet
took a toll

I tripped
and found myself
in Tibet

The infected leaves
of fall, crinkled
and left

Do you mind?

Who are you?
If I ran away for a week
would you notice?

I was feeling like sheep
I'm trying to learn
and hone my craft,
beat for beat,
so I can finally find
a piece of this Earth
that's truly *mine*

So let me ask you,
do you mind?

Tangerine Limbo

In the midst of limbo
Alone, yet his life
inside of a phone

Idle in the forest of my room
a life on paper
is so much more
pleasurable

It's too early to tell;
the boy picks
a Tangerine
underneath the
purple skies

While his insides
twists away
It's all the same,
such a shame

The midnight reds and greens
makes way
for the pinks and blues
of tomorrow

Don't dare to wallow
in forlorn's past
for I will be alright
tomorrow

Again

I don't want to sleep
the whole summer
away (again)

To leave the cosiness
behind, to deal with
the expectations of
the world

What a pain
to strive for mediocrity
rather than seek
something more

pass me by

we cross paths with people,
the stories they tell
we feel less alone
sparks fly, we're outside
the pink shell

the moon waning
the bells racing
as we pass
each other by
so let's try—

LATE BLOOMER

late bloomer

navigating
through relationships
not knowing
how to be honest

the calmest
i'll ever be
but it's your
corrosive touch—
that's flawless

to forgive
after acting
upon raw adrenaline
is the hardest

chunder

This is twenty-three
picking up the pieces
my heart chundered

Up until dawn,
dreading to start
the new day

I've been fiending,
barking up
the wrong tree

Whole intestines
wrapped up in my face;
I shudder then palpitate

diet soda

diet coke
and puppy eyes
the emeralds
the incas revered

staring at me
begging me
in knots
the bystander leered

overstayed

It seems that
I've overstayed
my welcome;
I didn't quite
know her

I've been trying
to hold on to
moments that
have passed me;
twice over

I fear that things
will change…
Yet in doing so:
I've changed

I've always wanted
to run away
But it always
takes me back
to rage

too tired

I'm too young to be rushing things
but too old to be wasting time

Finally old enough to do anything
but too tired to actually do it;
is it a crime?

And I'm the only one
holding myself back;
the bookkeeper's shoo-in
perpetuated through
Bonnie and Clyde

wallow

scared but
doing it anyway;
it's okay to wallow
but eventually
you have to stop
or you're gonna cry

smashed knee caps
i seldom pray
but filled my mind
with props
and paid my respects
within the Shinto shrine

FATHER TIME 'N' PLACE

Father Time 'n' Place

survivor's guilt

i left my soul back home
people out there are dying
while i'm over here feeling
survivor's guilt

ripping skin

i feel like i'm wearing
somebody's skin right now
i want to rip myself out:
grief, loneliness, impatience
i'm starting to go mad

father time

summer holidays
early starts
head heavy,
raw dreaming
in long rides and cars

building ikea wardrobes
instead of making art
picking weeds and roses
my hands are calloused
and marked

drive-thrus and mcmuffins
and eating in the car
longing to be alone
and far

away from my soul
and yet he's playing
his part

chalet

i'm still holding on to you
your expectations of me;
i was trying to live a life
you wanted for me

but i couldn't anymore
i was holding onto so much;
i was living for you,
and i can only do so much
against my own nature
to repay your debts

where did that lead me?
it led me closer to the abyss
than salvation and fortune;
the pressure from you was too much
and i'm sorry
but i chose myself

i'm still fuming
with the way you left;
at first we were like zombies,
then i started doing my own thing
and i chewed off my arm

i thought i got over you,
the grief, the pain:
i had to figure out who i was
after the storm;

early morning sprints

early mornings and after-hours
he rolls out of bed
to sprint to the bathroom floor

i lay down staring at the ceiling
i do not know who i am anymore

i'm with you
i don't want to talk about it

i hope you feel less pain
i don't want it to be about me

Staring

Scared to look death
in the eye

Haunted by my skellingtons
can't I survive?

I am too young for my hair
to grow out whites—

Death looming
and she's shy

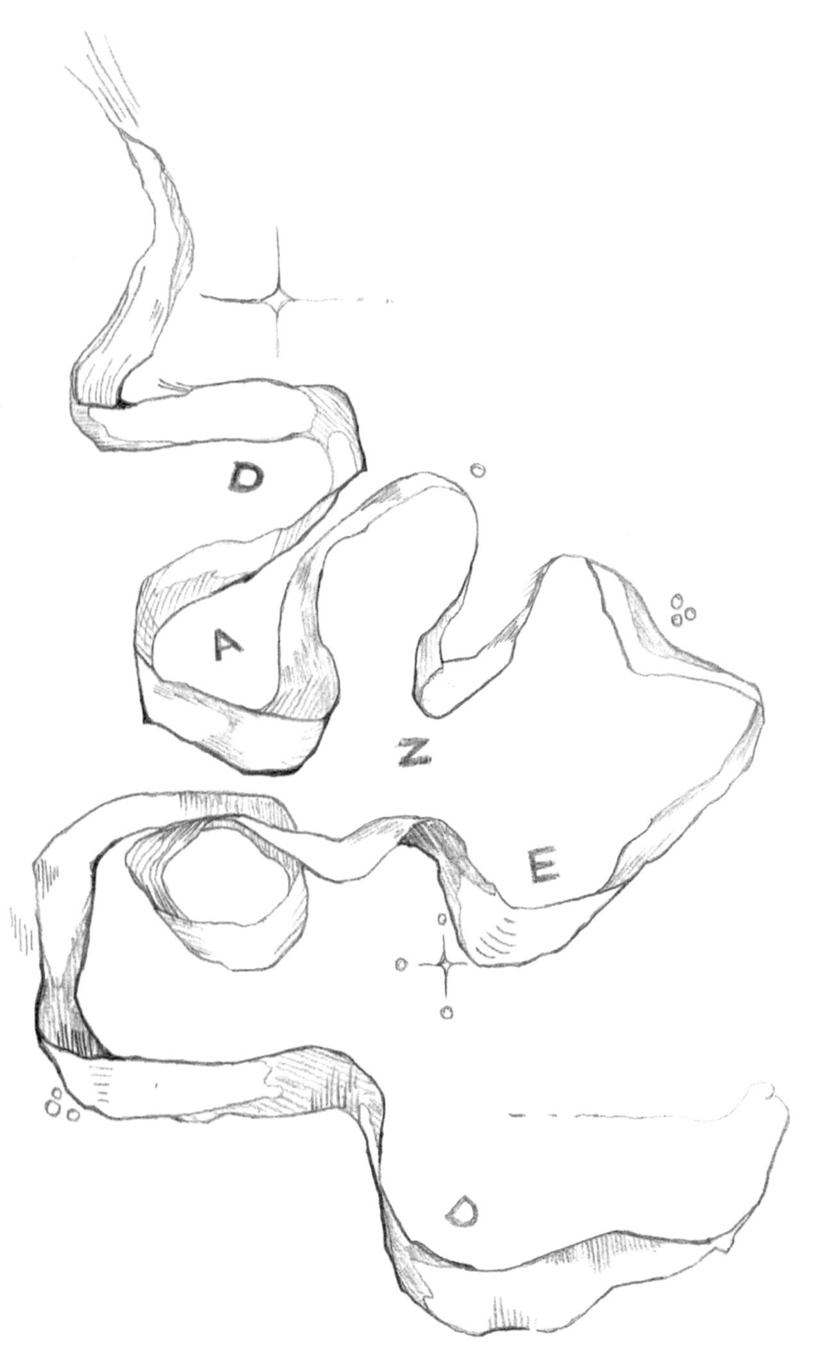
D
A
Z
E
D

Always in a daze

I spend my days
existing in the future
reminiscing the past
and always in a daze

Always afraid
(do I have a place here?)
stumbling to my own tempo

Guess this isn't the life
I've always dreamt off
Dad died
a couple of months ago

joey's purge

running out of time
dad's running out
of time

i'm scared to look
death in the eyes
i've already done
this before
wondering if i have the will
to survive

my soul shattered
i can't sleep anymore
one day i'll wake up
and he's—
fine?

Lying down on the floor helpless

Lying down
on the floor helpless

Desperate to get up
and take a bath;

Even if he has to crawl
there, but he's trapped

I lay down beside him,
so at least he's not alone

So careless in Atlanta,
I left my phone

Time bomb

someone next to me
is a ticking time bomb;
that's not very nice!

things just get worse
and worse
so insecure and
feeling left behind!

Late November

hiking through the valley
of the shadow of death
strolling through the beach
where my soul was kept

the turns and churns
of my stomach
how could people
live this way?

all my hopes and dreams left
one cold
late november evening
I awoke from a nap;
someone please take
my sorrows away

beam

lost dreams
with regrets
from the moment
i pry open my eyes,
was my life over?

beaming smiles
and mascots
that lie often;
i seem to sink lower

i'm right where I
dreamt of
is there more to life
than this?
i lay awake dreading tomorrow

need to get out of my shell
inner child curled up and cried
father slowly decaying
in the other room
what's the point?
i'm grinding down
my molars

dreaming (again)

yikes I've been dreaming again
(dreaming about us)

getting lost in
an italian train station again,
taking the wrong train up to the alps,
him stressing about getting lost;

dreaming about how
if you could see me now,
how proud you would be of me

i

i miss you so much
there's not a day
where i don't feel angry;
but i feel like maybe
i'm mistaking that anger
with grief

i haven't been able to cry
because when i feel any
sort of emotion
i stop myself
so as to feel nothing at all

i hope you know
that i've been doing well;
me and mum are doing great,
conquering our fears
and anxieties

but i've decided
to leave it behind
and let the pain go,
i'm sorry

i could've stayed
where i was
and have a life
you'd be proud of
but i'd rather chase
things that's never
been done
or thought of

i hope you'll understand

I'm glad I could say my goodbyes

I'm glad that I could say my goodbyes;
lying on the floor
craving a bubble bath
cleansed of this horrid state

I could see it in your eyes
mother's heart being torn
me… cowering in fear
I bring you shame

Now that I'm thinking about it;
I could unleash and serve
fury and wrath
dressed up on a plate

But I know
he wouldn't want that…
for now it remains untapped;
I'll be okay

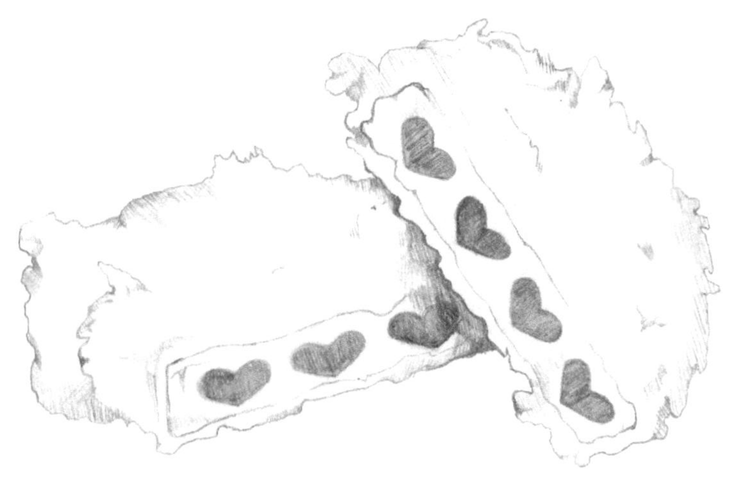

LOVE / とんかつ
TONKATSU

Love/Tonkatsu

runaway

Let's run away together
we'll never be this young

I wish u can see
That this won't last forever

I hope u know
That this love is mine to keep

dreaming of love

i live through my dreams:
a piece of my heart
taken once again;
i live a life
of companionship

my hair torn,
forlorn once again

motherly wishes

mother wishes
for me to sleep soundly
is it so hard
for you to see me?

to be hopelessly
romantic to others
is to be
hopelessly haunted

Fashion show

surrounded by blue faces
we're wearing prada

mancunians drinking pints
and wearing parkas

in a bodega
chopped cheese on a hero
i'd rather

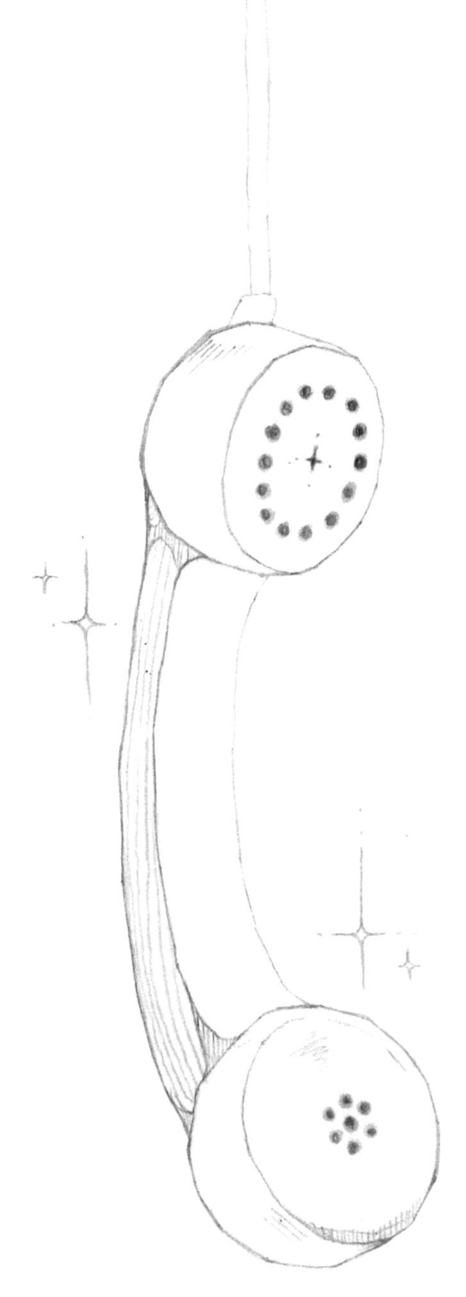

Maybe I'll say it

But you said it first!
You caught me by surprise,
and called me up late at night

You said—
and I asked you if you knew
who you were talking to

You said my name
and kept telling me that
You—

I have your attention

I don't care
about anyone else
when I'm
with you

My mind's blank
on everything else
but you

My senses
are overwhelmed,
they have your
attention

Unrequited love
once again—
but at least
I have an answer

Yearning
for companionship;
in the middle
of my
insufficient
ways

Better Call Saul

You told me
to tell you
(redacted)
otherwise
you'd cry

I didn't want to say it
because I would
have meant it

Feelings cut short
but maybe
I could court you;

We could read something,
we can go for a walk;
list all of the things
you want to hear

And maybe I'll say it

You've been good to me

You've been good to me
I'm so lost without you

It's just us two,
us against the world

I can't see the lilies
and you can't
see me

Feet swingin'

Feet swingin'
pointing towards the sheets

I'm fooled
by the empty streets

It's been a minute
let's meet

My midnight snack
we're here to feast

ame

nice to meet you
i'm currently bereaved
my viciousness
toward the end
was warranted
wasn't it?

still i can't stand
the way i dealt
with the aftermath
it's the same pattern

why do i never learn?
that false sense of control:
it's just an apparition
waiting to be reincarnated

24 hours

Why did you stay up
all night with me?
Why did you show me
your life in pictures?
Why did you say you love me?

Why am I overthinking this?
Why don't I love myself
first?
Why am I angry?

Why am I grieving?

Oh ~

waves

impatient
and jealous by nature
there are some natures
too noble to curb
and too lofty to bend

Saying goodbyes
isn't my forte
yet it hurts more;
the more I do it

Crossing paths
yet never going down
the same one—
just drifting away

I am not swimming
nor am I hiding
I'm just…
floating

I'm not giving myself
(space)
to come up for air,

Just know
I'm not waving
to say goodbye:

I'm just drowning

Novelty

What novelty is worth
that sweet
monotony:
where everything is known
and loved
because it is known?

It just so happens
I'm of middling
mediocre talent;
to some,
I've yet to show

And I'm from
the moon,
the stars,
and the sun

6:58 in Tokyo

6:58am
she asked me
if i regretted anything

she said
i put
"the burden of atlas"
on her soul

she doesn't know
or trust
me anymore

(i can't help myself)

she said i'm being selfish
but she's doing this
for herself

i woke up early
for this ~

champinjon

Nothing is what it seems
losing sight of the fact
that you don't see the fungus

Keeping quiet
is the greatest punishment
we can bring to ourselves

Yet the fallout caused
by ripping out the seams;

But to you
it's nothing—

You can say I was a day late,
but how could I?
I crossed the line didn't I?
I guess it was fate

I haven't been able to
breathe spores since

hallucinating

if i left and chased my dreams
would you still love me?
even if i'm as far away from you?
would you be okay momma?

Last Shenanigans

I've been thinking about you lately
our last shenanigans together
I hope you're doing well

Well you know what's scary?
Letting the fear make
all your decisions for you

accents

through my many lives
and in the deep depths of my soul
sometimes there's a pool of gold
but seldom moonlight;
i long for your fiery eyes
slipping and sliding
like a drowned woman
into the hot sky

i've worn orange socks
all the while, i'm full of pride
shopping for moccasins and coats
it moves! it's alive!
sent with all caps
handwritten note
like tides full facing
making me float

worried for miles ahead
rushing your pace
the day is done
before we get to bed;
together we arose
with moonlights buldging
and then slept with the sun

Blind

I just miss you

Looking through
(the looking glass)
I never realised
how much you cared for me

And it breaks my heart
to know how blind
I was to see
what you wanted to give me
and how much
blood, sweat and tears
you endured
just to put back that
smile on my face—
(I've lost since I was fourteen)

How blind and selfish was I?

Opaque Rainbow

she said I have the same eyes
as the rainbow…
she said it's tough for me to lie
especially with my smile…
because my eyes tell it otherwise

<3

The only way to find love
is to become it

Be the love
you wish to see

Love should be felt deeply
without the fear of getting rejected

Love that is hidden
is such a waste

In embracing love
you may encounter pain

Some people won't be able
to handle your love
and that's okay

Don't let one
or many
heartbreaks
define you

You can never say
the wrong thing
to the right person

Those who mind
don't matter
And
Those who matter
don't mind

Love requires truth
And
Truth is based on love

PORTRAITS

Portraits

bad omens

used to tell lies
but now my heart is open
i'm bad at saying goodbyes
i still linger in those moments

living my life
without bad omens
something to dream of right now
get out of your bag and call them

while you have the time
keep your heart open
keep me company;
won't you be mine?
remember your heart isn't broken

don't you dare lose your temper
remember that you still have time
what others think about your heart
isn't important
so long as you're having a good time

chicago blues

nothing to say
nothing to do
brain singing
the chicago blues

something inside me is bubbling up
i'm tired but my mind's racing
huh? my shoulder bruised

i need hands
please
pacing back and forth
my shoes squeaking

every second counts
i leave the crash site
spinal fluid leaking

shadow boxing

another day to fill me up
i'm a shadow of my former self
longing for some lovin'

      (to touch)
my bags under my eyes
can't you tell?

i'm slipping into filth
while you lay underneath:
we intertwine

and it's raining outside
yet the thunder
keeps us together

numb

i've been numbing myself lately
sleepless…
late nights
sleeping at 7am
"this is getting bad"

i miss my father
my mother's afraid
my mother's getting old

why has this made
my life,
            full of worries
why did i need to be in,
            the cold
why did she,
            shun me away

            from the ugliness
of life

why did she not want,
            to see me suffering

catch

all my past mistakes
are catching up to me
and it's been eating me
from the inside out

all of a sudden
i flip
i spiral
but i catch myself before
i fall

i have forgiven myself before
but lately i have been
alone
with the spiralling of thoughts
and apparitions of the past

it was written
but now i must forgive
and forget
because that's not me anymore

my past self scares me:
i didn't realise
that i would still be
concerned with these things
but i am

not perfect
but trying to be:
it feels futile

Head heavy

A lot going on,
in my head,
at the moment

I feel
like I can't
think properly

Head heavy
pen ready
stomach churning;
old habits
take a while
to shake off

there's death
looming
around the house
holding a glass of wine

Screams of:
horror,
shock, apathy

"Aren't you lonesome?"
Caught between limbo
once again

Stay put?
And what about my dreams?

Meditations

Breathe slow
and slowly let go
the crescent of your eyes
washes over me

And what is to
meeting new people
if you can't be present?!

The Cobbler

those shoes
they're missing soles
i invited you into my home
didn't make you out to be a mole
or maybe a sheep;
i haven't decided yet
it's few and far between

i didn't choose
my life to be like this
you chewed me up
with your mirrored mask
but who are you?
i can't believe
how people like you
can fake authenticity

you're trash
i helped you
settle in
and all i asked
is to reciprocate
my efforts;
it's insanity

how can you be
fake nice
in front of my mother?
the audacity
that pisses me off
more than anything

take of your shoes
and what do you bring?
maybe instead
you can look in the mirror;
where's your integrity?

i don't care what
the etiquette
or customs are;
you better bring
that fake two-faced
freak over
when i see you next

You see I'm all alone

You see
I'm all alone

Just stayed
in my room
and slept

Waiting
for something
to happen;
while potential
bled

The code broke
and they wept

butterflies and anguish

How do I make
the butterflies
and anguish
go away?

It's kinda
depressing
to realise
nothing's been
the same anyway

Institutionalised II

i'm tired all the time;
so alienated,

the weight of my dreams
crushing my shoulders
and the pressure to create

ya know?
i'm only getting older

Is there such a life worth living?

I'm sinking
Am I taking a leap of faith?
Or is it just luck?

I'm so selfish, I keep on taking;
She gives me a glance,
Turntable soul playing,
And now I'm taking off the chucks

Is there such a life worth living?

Spirits broken

Spirits broken
I hate being
stuck at home

So depressed
And now I'm ill
(so tired)

Yet I don't mind
being alone

vivid

everything inside
is shaken
the pressure to be alive;
to foster and attain
success is taken
in plain sight
but the pain
is familiar

no clue
if i'll thrive,
if i frame it
in a different light
maybe my aching
heart can finally rest;
yet it never seems
to dissipate

one lie
maybe can
shame me into
spiralling
or maybe a past
and futile memory

living vividly
in the past,
or dreading
the future

when i'm present
the void becomes more real
and it seems to grow

i wish i can escape:
even when i'm buried
in the sand

i know for a fact—
that i'll still feel the same

Thousand eyes

A thousand eyes,
watching, tracking,
hacking their way
into your life

Yet paralysed by
the boogiemen lurking
from within
the shadows;
preoccupied with
running out of time

A year of therapy
to deal with them
Can't you just leave me alone?
Let me live my life in peace!
And won't you move on?

Appreciate The Butterflies

Maybe I'm trying so hard so that I can be seen again
Ostracised from a tribe I once knew as home
I'm learning how to fail fast
Yet I fear failure
And you can't blame me for that

Maybe if I moved some place else,
the guilt won't catch up to me
Maybe if I make a lot of money,
the grief won't consume me
Maybe I shouldn't look for perfect,
because perfect should be looking for me

Indeed I'm just drowning myself
in lights and pixels,
smothering myself in cheap motels
with people I have no interest
in being with in the first place;
just to temporarily fill
the giant gaping
cosmic hole in my chest

Before I repeat myself like a broken record,
what should I do next?
I don't know
       I don't know
I feel like I don't have
any dreams anymore

Travelling to escape?
Or to find myself?
What's the difference?
I'll regret it

I'm putting all of this effort in—
just to prove you wrong;

These words charm
and offend people
So I'll just:

Appreciate The Butterflies ~

borrowed time

Time's moving too fast
I don't like it!
It's not fair
I've found home on this island
Yet it's cruel:
how I'll be leaving
all of this behind

My new life:
The loneliness doesn't go away
I can't really imagine a life outside of here

Borrowed time,
people will think,
my existence is a crime

Before I came here
I just wanted to sleep
the days away
without a care in the world…

Collisions

All these lives
keep me
in collisions

There are nights
where I am
haunted by apparitions

Past times
in exuberance
I was infatuated
with being in a rut

My mouth covered in lies
maybe I should have
kept my mouth shut;

To find myself in despair,
burning bridges
I had built

Without a care,
I lay awake,
the quack working
on my stitches;
I paid him a mil

humble

Oh! It's been a while
since I've picked up
a pen

In a thought loop:
all my anxieties
of the future
and all mistakes
of days past

These days humble me
covered in diseases,
lust, pride and fear

Avoiding the simplest things;
I haven't been outside,
self-flagellation
for fleeting connections

It was never real
(in the first place)
It was never written
(like Nas)
I should have left sooner

pools

vividly imagining a place
other than here:
pools of sweat
and tears
drip from my walls;
it's all i can hear

drowning my sleep
with oozing imagery
of toads at the flea
market;
hip hopping towards
the cakes

lashed out by traders,
that's the end of my trip—
i am the captain of my ship
and the master of my fate

Pamplona

Riding between Basque borders
of Spain and France
I know a moment like this
could never happen again:
my melted ice cream danced

For I am lucky to have you,
swirling pinks and dolphins
I never want this to end

Confessing our sins
and mistakes of days past
We're alright aren't we?
How long will we last?
Before their fins pass

guillotine

every saint has a past
and every sinner has a future;
slowly allowing myself
to receive grace

i've been angry
for the past five years
and i still continue to be:
tracing a putrid face

i let myself be…
slowly accepting
that not everything
should be planned out

i've achieved everything
that my fifteen year old self
had set out to do;
i now find myself
in limbo, waiting to be found

i don't have any dreams,
but i'm still seeking meaning;
i don't have a career,
but no one's hiring me;
i seek love,
but i'm blind to a mirror;
i seek stability,
but i thrive in the unknown;
i seek freedom,
but i'm anxious to put myself
out there

i have to make something
out of nothing… again
allowing for spontaneity
for cycles i need to depend

i'll allow myself to live,
to get my heart broken and
to break some hearts
do i have much to give?

who knows
maybe in the next five years
i'll have dreams again

Acknowledgements

I would like to thank Lisa, for her incredible illustrations and cover art. It has been a dream to finally collaborate with you, and an even bigger honour to share this creative journey as partners. You inspire me so much.

To my family and friends, I am profoundly grateful for your unwavering love and guidance. This book exists because of your constant encouragement and belief in me. You know who you are.

And to my readers, thank you from the bottom of my heart. Your continued support and focused attention, in a world full of distractions, mean the world to me

: -)

About The Author

Joey Groves is a British writer, poet, and co-founder of Grooovy, an independent creative studio that blends bold, expressive poetry with unique streetwear clothing design. At age twenty-one, Joey self-published his debut poetry book, Tangerine: Or, How I Learned to Trust the Process.

In 2020, he launched his first streetwear clothing line. The collection incorporated elements of the tangerine fruit, creating a cohesive visual identity that tied together his writing and fashion.

In addition to his work in writing and design, Joey has produced two lo-fi ambient albums, The Earlyman Tape and SCORPIO RABBIT, under the pseudonym 'Liddypool,' showcasing his versatility as a multidisciplinary artist.

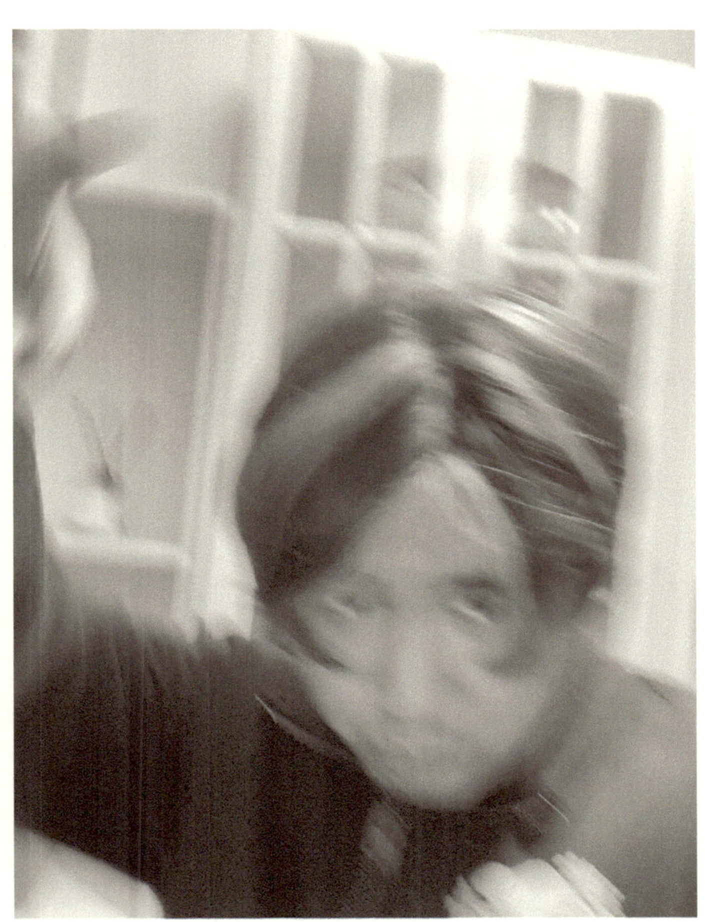

Gr
ooo
vy